# TRIUMPHANT RIDER

## THE
## LANCASTER
## ROMAN CAVALRY
## TOMBSTONE

STEPHEN BULL                    LANCASHIRE MUSEUMS

Published on behalf of Lancashire Museums, Stanley Street, Preston PR1 4YP
by Palatine Books,
an imprint of Carnegie Publishing
Carnegie House
Chatsworth Road
Lancaster
LA1 4SL
www.palatinebooks.co.uk

British Library Cataloguing-in-Publication data
A catalogue record for this book is available from the British Library

ISBN 1-874181-47-0
EAN 978–1-874181-47-7

Designed and typeset by Carnegie Publishing Ltd
Printed and bound in the UK by Alden Press, Oxford

# CONTENTS

# Acknowledgements

Lancashire Museums would like to thank all those associated with the recovery, research, purchase and conservation of the tombstone of Insus. These include Peter Noble at the Manchester University Archaeology Unit; Peter Iles, County Archaeologist; Professor David Shotter of Lancaster; Professor Alan Bowman and Dr Roger Tomlin at Oxford; Dr Paul Holder of Manchester; Heather Davis and Jenny Truran at Lancashire Conservation Studios, and Dr Jean Turnbull at the Centre for North West Regional Studies. We are also most grateful for the valuable advice and assistance provided by Dr John Paddock of the Corinium Museum, Cirencester, Tim Padley of Tullie House Museum Carlisle, Patrick Tostevin of Ribchester Roman Museum, Susan Fox at the Roman Baths Museum, Bath, Susan Hughes at the Grosvenor Museum, Chester, Dr Ralph Jackson at the British Museum, Dr Simon James, Dr Andrew White, Graham Sumner and Peter Clayton. Proofreading was provided by Natalie Kenneison. For financial support we are much indebted to the Heritage Lottery Fund; MLA-V&A Purchase Grant Fund, and the Haverfield Bequest.

A very special thank you is also due to Ben Edwards, Lancashire County Archaeologist during the period 1963–1995, who acted as consultant editor for this volume.

**Edmund Southworth, County Museums Officer**

# An Important Find

On the morning of 3 November 2005 Manchester University Archaeology Unit was undertaking what appeared to be routine investigations of a proposed development site near to the canal on Aldcliffe Rd, Lancaster, when a large slab of sandstone was struck by the mechanical digger. Its position suggested that it lay in what had once been a ditch near to the Roman road into Lancaster. Peter Noble, the dig director, had the stone turned over – and was greeted with the sight of a carving, which, after the removal of some of the dirt, showed a headless horseman. Being immediately aware that this could be of great significance, he quickly conferred with Peter Iles, County Archaeologist, and the decision was taken to contact Lancashire Museums with a view to getting what could be a major discovery out of the excavation, and under cover, away from the sleet and rain which was now beginning to fall. Later the same afternoon, under conditions of increasing cold, and the lens of a *Lancaster Guardian* photographer, the Lancashire Museums team arrived.

Remarkably, red dye or paint was still apparent highlighting the Latin inscription on the stone, and the image appeared virtually unweathered. The freshness of the carving suggested that the piece had toppled over into its inverted position not many years after it had been created, and that, despite its partial condition, it had not been moved for centuries. The first priority was a few quick photographs to ensure that the pigment evidence was captured, and that if disaster struck during delicate moving operations a record of the piece would remain. Next a brief on site conference ascertained that the digger, lifting

The Manchester University Archaeology Unit dig at Aldcliffe Road, near to the junction with Henry Street, Lancaster. Archaeological investigation was carried out because the old Roman Road, heading south from Lancaster, went through the site, and evidence of a cemetery had already been found nearby. Work was complicated by remains of later buildings including housing and a food depot. The massive main piece of the stone has just been turned over, presenting Peter Noble, standing with arms folded, with both an incredible find – and a problem of recovery.

gear, and tail lift of the van were all adequate to the task in hand – and that those doing the moving were properly equipped. The lift was then planned so as to minimise risk, both to the team and the artefact, with the stone being slung low over the ground surface with its attendants well clear.

Very carefully the heavy slab was now extracted from its resting place of almost 2000 years, and mounted on a nearby pallet. Next it was transferred from the slings onto the tail lift, and then into the waiting van. It was now apparent that what we had was about two thirds of the original artwork, and that if it had been broken here, or nearby, other parts might lie not far away. Though it was now getting dark, it was thought better to gather as much evidence as possible, rather than leave vital fragments on site over night. A finger tip search in the mud, using all hands of the archaeology and museum teams, soon located further smaller pieces – all at about the same depth, and within about a yard of where the first slab had lain. All appeared to be part of one layer, or context, reinforcing the idea that the stone had been broken *in situ*.

This work was made more difficult, not only by the weather conditions and gathering gloom, but by the fact that later walls had been built across the site, and one of these appeared to clip the corner of the position in which the stone had lain, face downwards. The obvious interpretation was that at some point in the past, perhaps in the eighteenth century, the site had been cleared to a certain depth to allow for the construction of housing. Luckily workmen of previous centuries had decided to leave the awkward and very heavy slab undisturbed and embedded beneath their new constructions, but now it meant

As sleet begins to fall, Graham Dowling, Senior Technician with Lancashire Museums, discusses the practicalities of moving the memorial with the Manchester unit digger operator. Aldcliffe Road lies just behind the fence visible on the right of the picture.

that the search for fragments had to extend up to, and just under, the old footings. Happily this was made possible, and relatively safe, by the fact that the old walls had now been truncated to a tiny fraction of their original height. One major piece of sandstone, already found nearby, showed evidence of having been worked, but bore no decoration. It was thought possible that this might once have been a base piece to the main part of the *stele* or stone, holding it stable in the ground when vertical. This, too, was retrieved and loaded.

One of the most promising lumps, however, was roughly half moon-shaped, and appeared to be of similar or identical material to that of the headless horseman. Eventually this piece was also turned over, and just enough of the mud was removed to reveal a head, wearing a splendid three plumed helmet. The face of a Roman cavalryman was then seen for the first time in two millennia. Given that fugitive paint or dye had been discovered earlier on the main fragment of the slab when it was first turned, it was decided that no on site cleaning of this second important portion should be attempted. In this way it was hoped to retain any additional paint or organic material which might have been preserved undisturbed, trapped away from air under the layer of dirt. Naturally Noble and his colleagues erred on the side of caution, collecting as many fragments of stone from the excavation as could be found. This approach meant that some material from an eighteenth century wall was also transported to Preston, but paid significant dividends in that, given time, and a better working environment, it proved possible to sift out and replace many pieces including a part of the horseman's cloak.

It was now apparent that the whole image showed a helmeted Roman horseman, face turned to the viewer, on a rearing stallion. Under the feet of the rider cowered a second, hunched, headless, figure, clutching sword and shield. Above the horseman's head was a sun symbol. Yet the most dramatic element was the rider's right hand: this not only held a sword,

but the hair of the defeated barbarian whose bearded head dangled below. Within a few days, further excavation by the Manchester team had secured not only more than 95% of the main tombstone, but at least one fragment of what is thought to be a second memorial. This can only represent a very small portion of a second stone, which is identifiable essentially through the inscription 'OXV'. This legend, thought to represent a number, prompted museum staff to dub it the 'Oxo Cube'. It is likely that the 'XV' is fifteen, whilst the 'O' is the final letter of a word such as 'anno' – being 'years old', or 'years of service'. Though overshadowed by the discovery of the magnificent and almost complete first slab, it is to be hoped that this second artefact may yield further information at a future date.

As the dig continued, it also became apparent that one or more ancient ditches and post holes were present on the site. At the time of writing these have yet to be fully interpreted, but

A moment of tension as Peter Noble, dig director, and Stephen Bull – backs to camera – watch the memorial clear the ground. The larger pieces were placed on pallets, before being moved across the site by the digger, this method being calculated to expose the pieces to minimum stress. (Picture by Peter Iles)

it seemed entirely possible that high status plots near to where the stone was found had been laid out as 'funerary enclosures'. What has not been discovered is any sign of a body: cremation was the usual Roman practice at this period, and the discovery of urns on nearby sites would also suggest that this was the fate of the mortal remains of Lancaster's cavalryman. If this is the case the slab is more strictly speaking a 'memorial' – for there is no evidence of a 'tomb'.

The main find was certainly of impressive dimensions, but ascertaining precise size and weight proved an inexact process for two main reasons. Firstly it was broken into fragments – secondly it was not obvious whether measurement should include the purported 'base stone', which might itself be incomplete. As a result early figures published in the media gave the original height of the memorial as anything between six and nine feet – or even two to three metres. As part of a preliminary condition report prepared in early December 2005 conservation officer Jenny Truran came to the conclusion that the 'top section' of the stone was 53 cm in height; the initial 'main inscribed fragment', 126 cm, and the maximum length of the 'base stone' 91 cm. In addition to the three major pieces, three other large, and 22 smaller, fragments were identified, though these would not materially alter the overall length and width calculations. The 'inscribed' portions together therefore came to 183 cm, and this is likely to be an approximation of the part which appeared above ground when the stone was erected. The total length of the entire stone could have been in excess of 270 cm, but this remains open to some conjecture. Its maximum width and thickness can be more exactly stated at 93 cm and 17 cm respectively. At some future date it is hoped

The fragment which suggests that a second stone was once present: a dressed piece of stone with the inscription 'OXV'.

that all the verified pieces can be taken to a weigh bridge or large balance. Until then weight has had to be estimated by the volume of material contained, working on the basis that sandstone is 2323 kg per cubic metre, or almost two and a half times the density of water. Very approximately therefore the memorial weighed 700 kg when first cut (about 1500 lb) – and, after historic damage and recent drying, somewhat less now.

Members of the Manchester team during photography at the Lancashire Conservation Studios. This view also shows the large 'base' fragment, and how small the 'Oxo cube' is in comparison.

# THE STONE AND ITS MEANING

The appearance of what was now assumed to be a graphically illustrated Roman inscription generated considerable excitement. The formal archaeological report will doubtless answer at least some of the many questions raised in greater depth, but it was soon possible to make some preliminary observations. Fairly obviously the slab was some kind of memorial, but it was not immediately apparent whether it was originally a single free standing stone, or part of a larger structure, or indeed who exactly was being commemorated. Consulting basic text books did however soon confirm that the slab was a 'tombstone' in the broad sense – of the general kind described as a 'Reiter' or 'rider' type: that is bearing a relief depicting a mounted cavalryman in action. Many, like the present example, show a fallen barbarian at the feet of the horse. Such *stelae* may hardly be described as common, but have been found in a number of parts of the Roman world. The greatest surviving concentration comes from the Rhineland, where about fifty have been noted. These memorials are uniquely military in character, have no obvious Roman precedent, and only a couple of rather untypical pieces have ever been identified in Italy. Some have associated the original concept of the 'rider' stone with Thrace, an area which approximates to parts of modern Bulgaria and Turkey, or even with Athens and ancient Greece itself. Until 1984 the most complete German catalogue noted just six more or less complete examples from the UK, plus a selection of partial pieces and lost fragments.

The German connection of this new find was reinforced by its inscription which included the phrase 'CIVE TREVER' — meaning citizen of the Treveri tribe, from the Trier area of Western Germany. The Treveri had fought both for and against the Romans, and had a fearsome reputation as mounted warriors: but their fortunes as an independent entity had declined after the failure of a rising, in 54 to 53 BC, in which they had fought against Julius Caesar. In 16 AD Trier became a Roman colony, and thereafter began to develop as a Roman city.

Heather Dowler, Assistant Keeper, Lancaster City Museum with Stephen Bull, Curator of Military History and Archaeology and the Insus memorial at Lancashire Conservation Studios, St Mary Street Preston, 14 November 2006. The stone is to be displayed in Lancaster City Museum.

In the weeks after its arrival at Lancashire Museums headquarters in Preston the stone was viewed by a number of prominent Romanists, archaeologists, and epigraphists. This distinguished body included Dr Roger Tomlin of Oxford; Professor David Shotter of Lancaster; Dr Paul Holder of Manchester; and Ben Edwards, former Lancashire County Archaeologist. Naturally one of the first matters to be considered was the inscription. The transcription of what is likely to become the standard version of the inscription was made by Dr Tomlin working with Dr Holder, and reads,

'DIS MANIBVS INSVS VODVLLI [...] CIVE TREVER EQVES ALAE AUG [.] VICTORIS CVRATOR DOMITIA [...]'

The translation for the key reference publication *Roman Inscriptions of Britain* is thus likely to be given as,

'To the shades of the dead. Insus son of Vodullus, citizen of the Treveri, cavalryman of the *ala Augusta*, troop of Victor, *curator.* Domitia his heir had this set up.'

The essential points, that this is the memorial of a Roman cavalryman of German origin, of the *ala Augusta*, an auxiliary unit, are universally agreed. A few alternative interpretations and nuances have however been advanced and are worth noting here. *Victoris,* for example, does not, in one word, translate literally as 'troop of Victor' – *Turma* being the usual word for a troop of horse, and the word *Turma* does appear in abbreviated form, for example, on the tombstones of Flavinus at Hexham Abbey, and of Dannicus at Cirencester. On the Lancaster stone a letter might be missing – but this is speculation. The grammar may not be strictly correct, but this leaves open some possibility that the intended meaning is that either the man commemorated or his unit 'is victorious' or 'victors' rather than 'Victor's'. Certainly the triumphant posture of the horseman might lend credence to such an interpretation.

There is also some discussion surrounding the use of the term 'curator'. This is commonly understood to mean a quartermaster non-commissioned officer, or junior officer of

One of the first pictures of the inscription on the stone as it lies in the mud, 3 November, 2005. Red dye or paint is still visible in the letters, giving some clue as to how it might have looked two thousand years ago.

Some of the key figures in the discovery, preservation and research into the Lancaster Roman tombstone, pictured at Lancashire Conservation Studios, 14 November 2006. Left to right, Peter Noble, dig director; Professor David Shotter of Lancaster; Peter Iles, County Archaeologist; Ben Edwards, and Edmund Southworth County Museums Officer.

the Roman army, in the way that we might now refer to, for example, a 'quartermaster sergeant' or 'supply officer'. The word survives complete in modern English, as for example in 'museum curator'. In either sense a 'curator' is a person who is the custodian of, or looks after, something. In the modern world this is likely to be museum collections, but in the Roman usage this could be military supplies for men or horses, or even the horses themselves. A Roman curator was thus a rather junior sort of appointment, but nevertheless one that required a degree of responsibility, and very probably numeracy and literacy. As Vegetius remarked, speaking of the legions, 'a number of offices on the establishment. . . require men of good education; examiners of recruits, therefore should not confine themselves to testing height, physical capacity and alertness, but should in certain cases take into account skill in writing and experience in arithmetic and book keeping'.

Sadly we lack any evidence from the stone as to the sequence of events regarding ranks, service, and the circumstances of the death of Insus. On the face of it the most likely scenario is that the man started as an ordinary horseman or 'eques', rose to a 'curator' – and then died or was killed. Yet it is also possible that the cavalryman was 'horseman' and 'curator' simultaneously, and that his death occurred after he had retired from active service. In this case the warlike depiction on the tombstone could be retrospective by several decades, and might have been funded by wealth gathered by Insus or his family from lands granted in the Lancaster area in recognition of his service. Nevertheless for various reasons, set out below, it is thought most likely that he died whilst still a soldier.

The formation to which Insus belonged to is given as the *ala Augusta*, an 'ala' being a 'wing' of a bird or army, and in this instance a unit of auxiliary cavalry. The use of the word 'wing' appears in this military sense to have been derived from the fact that when a major Roman force drew up in battle order the cavalry was commonly placed on the flanks, or wings, of the main body of infantry. The work of Dr Holder suggests that there were perhaps ten *alae* in Britain during the reign of the Emperor Trajan, and as many as 13 under Hadrian. Each *ala* is thought to have been comprised of either 500 or 1000 men, and was divided into 16 to 24 *turmae*, or troops, each *turma* being of 30 to 40 horsemen.

Yet our current knowledge of the identity and whereabouts of the auxiliary units of the Roman army is far from perfect, and depends largely upon inscriptions and diplomas – though it may yet be enlarged through the work currently being undertaken with the Vindolanda tablets, at the fort of the same name, near Hadrian's Wall in Northumberland. Indeed one reference to *ala Augusta* has already been identified from this source. That there was an *ala* at Lancaster was already suspected from a partial inscription found in 1772 during the digging of a cellar in Pudding Lane, and since lost. This earlier piece commemorated Lucius

Julius Apollinaris, a 30 year old horseman of the Treveri, and the presence of two cavalrymen from Trier in Lancaster seems to fit together remarkably well.

This seemingly conclusive set of observations is complicated by the fact that there was more than one *ala Augusta* in Roman Britain. There are references, for example, to an *ala Augusta Gallorum Petriana* – an august Petrian wing of Gauls, and an *ala Augusta Gallorum Proculeiana* – an august Proculeian wing of Gauls. An *ala Augusta Vocontiorum* – the august wing of the Vocontii, is thought to have been first in Lower Germany, appearing before AD 122 in Britain. A unit referred to as the *ala Augusta ob virtutem appellata* – 'named Augustan by reason of their virtue' is recorded as the first garrison of Chesters fort on Hadrian's wall. The regimental history is thus somewhat tortuous and open to a number of possible interpretations. Some scholars have suggested that the unit in the Lancaster area in which Insus served was the *Augusta Gallorum Proculeiana*, others that the *Augusta Vocontiorum* is more probable. Just to confuse matters further an inscription referring to the bath house at Lancaster mentions that it was restored for the use of the 'Sebosian cavalry' and the *ala Augusta Sebosiana* – an august wing of Sebusiani – did serve in Germany early in their existence. An altar from Weardale certainly records the presence of the commander of the *Sebosiana* in the north of England, and a local station for the unit is similarly attested by stamps on tiles. A 'Reiter' stone relating to a former soldier of the *Sebosiana* was also found at Worms on the Rhine. This is somewhat similar to the Lancaster stone, but differs in workmanship and details of composition. It includes for example a *calo*, or servant, a feature seldom, or never, found on British pieces depending on interpretation of the surviving evidence.

Another possibility yet to be explored is that as a title 'Augusta' is in itself fairly nebulous, being applied as we might prefix a modern unit 'Royal' or 'Prince's' – something which might be granted or withdrawn according to politics or

The jigsaw completed.
An overall view of
the main portion of
the memorial to Insus
with the broken pieces
arranged in the correct
places.

performance over time. In the light of such an interpretation the tribe or area becomes the more significant part of the unit designation making the *Sebosiana* or the *Vocontiorum* the most likely contenders given the German connections of the Lancaster horsemen. One other intriguing possible explanation is that the actual title of the unit on the new Lancaster stone should be read as *ala Augusta Victoris* and thus we would have the title of a new and hitherto unknown unit – 'the august and victorious' wing of auxiliaries composed of Treveri.

This much is exciting enough, and the sort of information that we might hope to glean in the rare event of the discovery of a 'Reiter' stone. What appears to make the Lancaster tombstone unique internationally however is the depiction of the human forms. Most 'Reiter' figures are sculpted with spear and shield – this example wields a sword. Most spectacular however is the gruesome detail of the barbarian, for this figure is not merely prostrate, but decapitated. More intriguing still is that his bearded head is clutched by its hair by the victorious cavalry figure. The only obvious parallels are not on funerary monuments, and would appear to be figures on the celebrated Trajan's Column, and the Bridgeness slab from the Antonine wall, discovered in 1868, which includes a decapitated barbarian. Some German Reiter stones, and examples from Kirkby Thore and Chesters, show swords being brandished, but no actual decapitation.

The headless state of both the rider and his enemy when the stone was found generated a good deal of speculation. One theory suggests that the Lancaster stone was deliberately thrown down, and the rider's head broken off, as an act of deliberate subversion or vandalism, designed as a symbolic blow against the occupier. In this there are parallels with similar ideas raised about the tombstone of Longinus at Colchester. In the case of Longinus it was thought that the memorial was toppled during the Boudican revolt, leading to the breaking off of the face. The main part of this memorial was discovered by workmen in 1928, but the face was not recovered by archaeologists until 1996, and the parts were finally reunited in 2006. Sadly for this romantic story it would now appear that at least part of the damage to Longinus was inflicted in modern times, not antiquity. Another interesting theory, advanced primarily by Professor Shotter, is that the removal of the barbarian's head in the image is an echo of Druidic or other native religious practice in the form of 'head cults'. Certainly a

Detail of the slightly later Bridgeness 'distance slab' from the Antonine wall in Scotland, showing a parallel to the decapitation depicted on the Lancaster tombstone.

number of 'bog bodies' from the bronze and iron ages show evidence of decapitation, as do some burials from the Roman era in Britain. Whatever the case the beheading of Insus after death, and his headless historic adversary, make the Lancaster stone one of the most vivid contemporary depictions of Roman Britain in existence.

Apart from his decapitated condition, the fallen barbarian with his sword and shield is reminiscent of many of the other British and Continental Reiter stones. His position of abasement, crumpled, small, and partially naked is deliberate. The beard and long hair on his decapitated head may have been accurately observed from enemy Britons, but in any case is well calculated to show his barbarism and uncivilized status. His abject defeat

Detail showing the hunched body of the barbarian with the booted foot of Insus resting on the small of his back.

is further emphasised by the foot of Insus which appears to rest on the small of his back. Whilst the barbarian is clearly insignificant compared to the triumphant rider, his image is still carefully executed. Viewing the barbarian figure from an oblique angle shows that he has been modelled in three dimensions, with two buttocks and two feet, even though these are not readily apparent when the scene is viewed full on.

Though not as extensive as those on the memorial to Longinus, the decorative features around the somewhat asymmetrical top of the Lancaster stone are impressive and appear to contain a number of allusions to the life, death, and religion of Insus. The face in the sun figure at the apex of the stone may be just a stylised sun, but might also be interpreted as either a symbol of Mithras, a God venerated by Roman soldiery, or as the head of a Medusa. The 'S' shapes in the embellishment which runs down either side of the top portion of the stone are readily apparent. Less obvious is the foliate decoration, the leaves of which appear to represent laurel and oak – both of which are redolent of victory and military valour. Oak leaves in particular have remained a symbol of military bravery in both modern Britain and Germany.

Initially it was unclear where the raw material from which the Lancaster stone had been carved was quarried. Some scholars fancied that it must have been imported, others that it must have travelled some distance within the UK. One or two parties ventured the opinion that it was much easier to move a stonemason than a ton of sandstone, and therefore the rock was more likely to be local. In an attempt to settle this dispute two geologists were independently approached for an opinion as to the origin of the stone. There was broad agreement – with one stating that the rock was from within 25 miles of Lancaster, with the other suggesting that it was from a point much closer still. It therefore seems reasonable to conclude that the stone was quarried locally, whilst the hands that carved it could have belonged to a mason who travelled with the Roman army.

It is interesting to note that the lettering and the image on the stone do not appear to be of an even or equal quality. The portrayal of the horseman is bold and dramatic, whilst the lettering is oddly spaced and rather cramped. A number of possible reasons for this have been suggested. Perhaps the most obvious explanation is that the picture and the legend have been executed by different craftsmen, and that the person carving the words was only semi-literate. It is also difficult to rule out the possibility that the dramatic picture of the horseman was created first – as a generic memorial to a cavalry officer – then the specific inscription could have been added subsequently.

Some memorial effigies were coloured at the time of their erection. This interpretation of Insus is by Dr Simon James of Leicester University. Note that in this version possible missing parts of the inscription have also been restored.

# THE ARMS AND EQUIPMENT

One of the most valuable aspects of the Lancaster stone is that it appears to give us a clear snapshot of the arms and equipment of a Roman auxiliary cavalryman, acting as a non-commissioned or junior officer. Whether the carving is an accurate portrait, like a modern photograph, is open to question — but it is likely that the equipment depicted would have been familiar to the contemporary viewer. It is also probable that it is similar enough to that worn by Insus and his unit for his comrades and family to identify with this martial image.

The first point worthy of note is that Insus is depicted with a sword: most other similar images have a spear. In the British context Sextus Valerius Genialis and Dannicus at Cirencester; Rufus Sita at Gloucester; and the unnamed figure at Ribchester for example, all have spears. Flavinus at Hexham holds a staff or standard. Longinus at Colchester now has nothing in his right hand, but it is thought that he was once armed with a spear. The sword of Insus has an appearance of considerable width, and short length, being reminiscent of a *gladius*, the weapon mostly used as a thrusting weapon by Roman infantry. Surviving archaeological examples of such swords have blades in the range of about 35 to 60 cm in length, and have popularly been divided into two major groups, the 'Mainz' type with a tapering blade and long point, and the later 'Pompeii' type with parallel edges, and short point. By general appearance we might therefore define the sword of Insus as a 'Mainz type' *gladius* — a form

Example of a 'gladius' from Germany, first century AD. This weapon is traditionally associated with the infantry. (After Ulbert, 1969)

The 'spatha': the proportionately long and narrow type of sword usually carried by the auxiliary cavalry.

which was gradually being replaced in the second half of the first century AD. The fact that Mainz in Germany is relatively close to the native area of the Treveri may not be a coincidence.

What is slightly puzzling about this deduction is that we might have expected an auxiliary cavalryman to have been armed with a *spatha,* the long sword of many of the tribal peoples of Western Europe, an arm especially suited to use on horseback by virtue of its considerable reach. Such weapons are also strongly associated with Germany, and the Rhine and Danube regions. Archaeological examples of *spathae* have a relatively narrow width to length ratio and often have blades in the range of about 60 to 90 cm long. On the basis of this evidence we might advance an hypothesis that either Insus was particularly Romanised, or that the carrying of short swords was usual for quartermasters and non commissioned officers who might be expected to discharge many of their duties dismounted. This may however simply be a question of artistic depiction and definition – though well formed three dimensionally, nothing in the relief is particularly well represented in terms of scale, and the somewhat arbitrary nature of length distinctions might suggest that in fact we are looking at a very short *spatha,* not a long *gladius.* In this context it is worth noting that the sword carried by the fallen barbarian is similar to that borne by Insus, having a flattened looking globular pommel and a cross piece that extends just fractionally beyond the width of the blade. It is also wide in terms of the proportionate length of the blade to the grip and other fittings.

Both Insus and his foe carry substantial shields with rounded tops, though that of the barbarian has more of a 'playing card' shape. A portion of the inside of each shield is presented to the viewer. How the cavalryman is holding his is unclear, due in part to the position of his mount's head and ear, but we can see that the barbarian is manipulating his by means of a roughly transverse central grip. The barbarian shield thus bears at least some superficial similarity to an example made of wooden planks, bound with leather, found at Clonoura, County Tipperary, in the Republic of Ireland. Very little can be adduced about the shield carried by Insus except to remark that some auxiliaries depicted on Trajan's column carry rather more oval types, whilst some legionaries from the altar of Domitius Ahenobarbus in the Louvre have large shields with a rounded top section. There are round topped, or oval, shields shown on other British Reiter stones, including those to Longinus; Rufus Sita; and Dannicus. The Ribchester rider has a straighter top edge to his shield, though it still has a slightly curved appearance. The remains of an oblong shield with rounded ends, thought to be the shield of an auxiliary dating from the first century, was found in the fort at Doncaster, and may therefore be of a similar type.

Detail of the memorial to Insus son of Vodullus: showing the head of the rider with the splendid plumed auxiliary cavalry helmet, and the sun symbol at the apex of the monument.

The rider's splendid helmet might well be described as of the Auxiliary Cavalry 'A Type' as identified by the late Russell Robinson in his *Armour of Imperial Rome*. It has large, all enveloping cheek pieces, and a brow reinforcement. This general design was apparently fairly common in the first century, and is represented by two examples and some fragments in British collections. One helmet was retrieved from the fort at Newstead in Scotland, and dated to about 100 AD, the other came from Northwich, Cheshire. Neither is in perfect condition, although it has been observed by Dr Paddock, that more complete examples have been identified on the continent, notably at Xanten, Koblenz-Bubenheim and Weiler – with the result that in Germany that this type of headgear is known as the 'Weiler Type'. Such helmets of iron were

An idea of how the stone of Insus will look when the fragments of the image and inscription have been rejoined. The stone is likely to be displayed in this form: conserved, cleaned, and reassembled but without any reconstruction of lost elements.

commonly covered with a copper alloy embossed to look like hair – a feature clearly visible on the Northwich example. If the image on the tombstone was originally covered with gesso and painted, or otherwise coloured, other details of armour and helmet might well have been picked out.

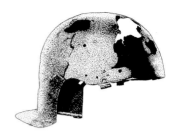

The helmet of the 'Weiler' type found at Newstead.

The helmet appears to have a central, stiff, brush-like crest with plumes or bushy feathers mounted so as to droop over on either side, like horns. Though not identical this brings to mind the helmet worm by Flavinus at Hexham, which appears to be fitted with feathers. Triple plumes or crests were by no means limited to the auxiliary forces, or to a narrow historical date range. The Greek historian Polybius is quoted in Sir James Turner's *Pallas Armata* (1683) as suggesting that triple feathers, of red or black, standing straight up, 'one and a half feet high' were a general mark of the Roman soldier's helmet as early as 150 BC. A Roman soldier figure executed in relief on a block of sandstone, now at Whalley church, Lancashire, has headgear with three plumes and has been identified as a depiction of Mars. Other 'horned god' figures of various dates, with two or three horns or crests, later became conflated with Christian notions of devils, and even 'lords of misrule' and jesters.

For anyone who might still believe that all Roman soldiers wore open sandals and skirt-like nether wear, the image of Insus is good evidence that in northern climes the soldier's clothing was commonsense and well adapted to bad weather. Working from the feet upwards, the rider wears short boots, probably some form of sock or stocking, and breeches. If the boots are accurately depicted they have a fairly soft, flexible form, well suited to mounted use. The breeches also have a practical sort of appearance for riding, and come down to just below the knee. They bring to mind Arrian's reference to the 'tight' trousers of Roman horsemen on parade, whose leg wear was noticeably closer fitting than that of 'Parthians and Armenians'. On the top half of the rider's body is worn a long sleeved, thigh length, tunic. This is most likely to be of cloth, but a leather garment with some defensive property, or flexible armour, cannot be ruled out. There is no obvious front closure, so it may be of a type pulled on over the head. What happens at the cuff is uncertain: the feature on the right wrist could conceivably be some form of bracer, or bracelet, but equally may represent a sleeve turn back which could be pulled down in inclement weather. Surprising as it may seem long sleeved tunics with cuffs were not unknown in the Flavian period. What may be a leather strap or baldric to support a scabbard runs over the rider's left shoulder and down over his right hip.

Over the whole ensemble the rider wears a *sagum* or cloak, again a very practical garment – and military riding cloaks continue to be worn by a few units right up to the present day. This example, which billows out behind the fast-moving rider, is closed on the chest by what appears to be a roughly circular, large floriate brooch, or fastening. This is interesting as work on Roman brooches by Margaret Snape suggests that 'plate' and penannular types are proportionately more common in the archaeological record of the north of England. This discrepancy in distribution may be related to the fact that the north was essentially a 'military' zone for much of the period, whilst the south was far more 'civilian'. In any case a heavy cloak fastener, or clasp, would have had to be a much more robust item than a decorative brooch. Interestingly the riding garments shown on the memorial are paralleled in the Vindolanda tablets of the same period, where there are references to cloaks, tunics, and some form of coat. Whether the dress worn by the figure of Insus in the relief might constitute a 'uniform' is a matter of debate. Evidence relating to the legions certainly shows deductions for the supply of *vestimentis* or clothing: but what auxiliary cavalry had to supply themselves, or were given, is less clear. Even so Dr Webster is on record as having suggested that though the *auxilia* never became standardised, 'it is probable that each regiment had its own distinctive features, which once established were jealously guarded'.

Vegetius tells us that mounted troops of the *alae* were supposed to be at least 1.72 m (or just over five feet seven inches) in height. Compared to this sort of stature the cavalryman's mount appears exaggeratedly small. Doubtless this is in part an accident of artistic style, and the need to depict a horse, usually a long beast, on a stone that is taller than it is wide. Nevertheless bone analysis of horses of the Roman period does suggest that the breeds of this period were in general somewhat smaller than animals of the modern era. The horse furniture of the steed is interesting, and requires some explanation. As we would expect, there are no stirrups to be seen, these only coming into use at the end of the Roman period. From the early Empire onwards lack of grip and balance was therefore usually compensated for by use of a horned saddle which gave the rider a firm seat. Frustratingly the depiction of Insus does not show us whether any saddle, or of what sort, is being used – though the rest of the harness would appear to imply that one was intended to be imagined by the viewer. Lines around the front of the seat of the rider represent a large saddle cloth, the bottom portion of which appears to end in elaborate decorative strips, or possibly hanging triplet straps, about the belly of the animal. A breeching strap goes around the rump of the horse in such a way as may suggest the presence of an unseen crupper, running down the back of the animal to its tail. At the haunches short decorative straps are shown with some sort of finial, which may represent metal strap ends or even bells. At the fore end the breast strap of the animal is broad and decorative, patterned as though to show plaiting or decorative embossing. The head harness is clearly depicted with a wide band, or hackamore, around the muzzle. However the reins appear to represent something of an anomaly, as they hang down low on the horse's neck, making it difficult to imagine how Insus can simultaneously be holding his sword, shield, and trophy head, as well as maintaining control of his horse.

Bronze statuette of a cavalryman, from Saalberg, Germany. (Russell-Robinson, 1975).

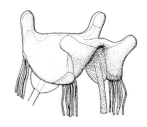

A Roman military saddle showing the distinctive 'horns' which held the rider in his seat. (After a reconstruction by P. Connolly)

Artist's impression of Insus son of Vodullus, citizen of the Treveri, Curator, Auxiliary Cavalry, northern England, c. 80 AD, by Graham Sumner.   In this painting a number of points not clear in the surviving stone effigy have been interpreted to create a complete picture showing how Insus might have appeared in life. Here it has been assumed that, like several other figures of the period, the rider wore armour. Mail certainly existed, being in use by the fifth century BC. The sword has been reconstructed as a form of spatha – a weapon familiar to the German tribes and Roman auxiliaries. Its length made it more suitable for mounted use than the infantry sword. The triple decorations of the helmet are shown here as a red central crest flanked by white feathers: an arrangement influenced by the feather plumes seen on the roughly contemporary image of Flavinus. Details of the saddle and shield have been filled in from other Roman examples.

# DATING THE TOMBSTONE

The stone bears no clear date, such as the year of the emperor's reign in which it was erected. Yet circumstantial and stylistic evidence, as well as the form of the epitaph, give us an approximate idea of its antiquity. Julius Caesar had first mounted expeditions to Britain as early as 55 BC and 54 BC, but the Roman soldiers neither stopped long, nor penetrated far beyond the Thames. Systematic conquest began only after the invasion of Claudius in 43 AD, but even then it took time to reach the outer parts of what is now England, and it is probable that some of the first Roman incursions into the North West were via the estuaries of the Ribble, Lune, and Mersey. Major campaigns in these parts were finally mounted under the jurisdiction of Roman governors Cerialis and Agricola during the period AD 71 to 83, with specific actions against the local people of the Brigantes known to have occurred in 78 AD. The large fort at Lancaster, which once occupied the present site of the castle, and land to the north, was probably first constructed at about this time, as was the fort at Ribchester. After the departure of Agricola the North West was gradually consolidated, and several forts built during his time were enlarged or improved, but peace did not last indefinitely, and there were intermittent episodes of rebellion, and war. The accession of Hadrian in 117 was coincident with further outbreaks of rebellion, but the frontier with what is now Scotland was ultimately stabilised by the building of the new Emperor's famous wall.

Many of the surviving British Reiter stones are dated to the first century AD, with Longinus, for example, pre-dating 60 AD. Flavinus, the Hexham Abbey memorial, has been placed at about 70 to 90 AD. Whether Insus died in service, or expired as a rich old man several decades after his military exploits, could in theory make his memorial somewhat later, though on the basis of existing evidence this is dubious. One clue that the death of the Lancaster cavalryman occurred during his soldiering career is his name. Retired auxiliaries were entitled to Roman citizenship, and usually adopted the *tria nomina* – or three part name consonant with this status. Insus lacks this distinction, and is therefore unlikely to have completed his military service prior to his death. Furthermore Schleiermacher suggests that veterans were usually identified as such, and were often commemorated by distinctive memorials. This may be circumstantial, but since the stone of Insus is not explicitly that of a veteran, and not that of a Roman citizen, it could be taken to suggest death in service. In such a scenario he would have been between about 20 and 40 at the time of death.

We also know that a number of auxiliary *alae* were in the North West of England towards the end of the first century, and during the second. Perhaps most famously, units of Asturians and Sarmatians have been identified with the cavalry fort at Ribchester. Similarly an *ala Augusta* has previously been associated with the area, as for example in the work of Ben Edwards and Professor David Shotter. The Reiter memorials from Chester are later, dating between the second and fourth centuries. It may tentatively be suggested therefore that the Lancaster piece was created some time between about AD 75 and AD 120, with the most likely date being prior to 100 AD. This would certainly accord well with many of the features shown in the image, as for example the long sleeved tunic; horse furniture; types of sword and helmet, and other detail.

Both stylistically and geographically the closest parallel to the memorial to Insus is the Reiter stone displayed at the Ribchester Roman museum. This lacks any inscription, and

Overall view of the relatively unkown Ribchester 'Reiter' stone. Its style and composition strongly suggest that it is a companion piece to the stone of Insus found at Lancaster. (Ribchester Roman Museum Trust)

Detail of the rider shown on the Ribchester stone, showing the disc shaped cloak fastener and the rider's head which lacks any helmet. (Ribchester Roman Museum Trust)

Horses head detail from the Ribchester stone. The ear position, and detailed execution of the features shows strong similarities with the horse depicted on the Lancaster stone. (Ribchester Roman Museum Trust)

 32

does not appear in the Schleiermacher catalogue *Romische Reitergrabsteine*. According to the Ribchester museum it was discovered in 1876 and not recovered under any controlled archaeological conditions. Since Asturian auxiliary troops were based in the vicinity it has been deduced that this rider may be an Asturian – originally a native of North West Spain – though any documentary proof of this attribution is lacking. This figure is bareheaded, and equipped with a spear, but in many other respects has points of likeness to the Lancaster rider. The treatment of the horse is startlingly alike, having its ears in the same position, a similar mouth, tail, and eyes, and a hoof which appears to break the frame of the composition. The cloak of the Ribchester soldier is executed in a generally comparable fashion with a fastener similar, to, though not as elaborate as, that worn by the Lancaster figure. By way of experiment Ben Edwards has made drawings of both figures. When one is superimposed upon the other the back half of both horses is almost coincident, whilst the sweep of the belly, head, and one front leg are also revealed to be posed in an almost identical manner.

It may be speculated that the hand that carved the memorial to Insus and that to the Ribchester rider are one and the same. Even if they are not, it is beyond reasonable doubt that they came from the same stylistic tradition, and are not far from each other in terms of date. What is also very likely is that the Ribchester figure with spear, no helmet, and less ornate equipment, is more typical of the ordinary auxiliary *eques*, whilst Insus with his sword, helmet, multiple plumes and other embellishments is evocative of officer, or at least non commissioned officer, status. As in the Roman tradition both *Eques* and *Curator* of the auxiliaries would have been regarded as superior to their infantry equivalents.

# Reiter Tombstones from Roman Britain

- ● REITER WITH ADVERSARY (GEGNER)
- ✦ REITER WITHOUT ADVERSARY (GEGNER)

STANWIX

CHESTERS
HALTON CHESTERS

CORBRIDGE (?)

MARYPORT

KIRKBY THORE

LANCASTER

?KIRKHAM

RIBCHESTER

CHESTER

WROXETER

GLOUCESTER

COLCHESTER

CIRENCESTER

BATH

DORCHESTER

0    MILES    100

0    KM    100

# The Stone Acquired
# and Conserved

Press stories soon speculated that the tombstone might be sold abroad – with a piece in *The Times* of February 9th 2006 suggesting a likely valuation of anything up to $100,000. In March, *British Archaeology* ran a story under the headline 'Unique Roman Tombstone May Leave UK'. Many internet web sites and 'blogs' were also alive to the issue, with contributors as far away as Canada adding to a heated debate. Naturally it was generally thought vital that such a piece should remain in Britain, preferably locally and in the public domain: but this was not the sort of money that any local museum service could expect to find in a hurry, and so concerted efforts to put together bids to funding bodies were urgently required. The need for immediate action was further fuelled by the news that the stone was the subject of an application for an export licence. At this stage the discovery of Insus became a matter of great public interest as well an archaeological issue, with Ian Barker, Leader of Lancaster City Council writing to Tessa Jowell, Secretary of State for Culture to ask for the refusal of the export licence. Similar representations were later made by Lancaster and Wyre MP, Ben Wallace, to David Lammy. One Roman army enthusiast wrote direct to the Queen, imploring her to intervene directly in her capacity as Duke of Lancaster. This missive was later also forwarded to the Secretary of State with an endorsement from the Palace.

Thereafter detailed negotiations with both a range of grant making bodies and the owner of the site were required to

(Opposite) Distribution plan of the known 'Reiter' stones – most are from the western side of England, which is interesting since in later centuries the east of England was regarded as better cavalry country. This western oriented distribution may have something to say about either Roman campaigns, or survival rates of evidence on this side of the country.
(Ben Edwards).

Detail of the Lancaster stone showing the fallen barbarian with sword and shield.

put together a package acceptable to all the interested parties. With such complex matters at stake, discussions were necessarily protracted – but a common desire to see Lancaster's premier archaeological find of recent times made available to the public, in the town where it had rested for two millennia, was soon identified. An initial agreement was therefore reached under which the stone would be kept at Lancashire Museums headquarters in Preston until such time as it had dried out and negotiations were concluded. Whilst it was here the Manchester archaeologists, Roman specialists, conservators and geologists would have the chance for study pending display at a suitable venue in Lancaster. Happily funds to secure the stone were successfully raised in the year following the find, the Haverfield Trust, V&A MLA Purchase Grant Fund, and Heritage Lottery Fund being prominent contributors. A crucial ingredient in the lottery funded work is to be a new full length study, published in association with the Centre for North West Regional Studies, encompassing all the Roman cemeteries of Lancaster, to be edited by Professor Shotter and Peter Iles. This volume will include not only the latest thought on the tombstone itself, but a synthesis of all the archaeological work on Lancaster's Roman cemeteries – much of which has been conducted by Oxford Archaeology (North) and the Manchester University unit in recent years.

A public announcement of the successful acquisition of the memorial to Insus was made by Edmund Southworth, County Museums Officer, at the Lancashire Conservation Studios, in

Preston, on the morning of 14th November 2006. This was greeted with similar media interest to the early news of the discovery, and in addition to extensive press and radio coverage members of the team responsible were interviewed on BBC TV's 'North West Tonight' regional news. In the following days and weeks the fame of the head hunting Treveri spread far and wide, through many publications and web sites, including that of the '24hour Museum' – and across into North America, and Australia, thus reaching continents unknown to Europeans when the cavalryman was alive.

Drying the memorial took several months after the discovery, during which the surface hue lightened to a pale sandy colour. At the time of writing the stone of is undergoing conservation at the Lancashire Conservation Studios. This work is likely to include cleaning any remaining mud, and then the joining of the various parts. The plan for the larger pieces involves the insertion of aluminium rod, whilst smaller pieces can be attached using a reversible adhesive resin process. The use of a rod, or rods, is the most controversial and ticklish part of the process, for whilst this will provide a secure join making safe public display in an upright position practicable there is likely to be some small scale, internal, damage to the fabric of the stone which is not reversible. Conversely it will provide small samples of the rock which can be tested without damaging the outward appearance and integrity of the piece. A useful guide, for both conservators and others who wish to see the stone as complete as possible before display, has been the photographing and 'digital' joining up of the resulting image. It is anticipated that the memorial of Insus, son of Vodullus, will be put on permanent public display at Lancaster City Museum during early 2008, with the publication of the full archaeological reports for the Roman cemetery sites of Lancaster later in the year.

An altar from Corbridge recording an action against the Corionototae by the prefect of cavalry.

LONGINVSSDAPEZE
MATYCII DVPLICARIVS
ALAPRIMAI ACVMPA
SARI ANNO XL AI ORVM XV
HEREDES EXS TES TA

# THE REITER STONES OF ROMAN BRITAIN

## COMPLETE, OR NEAR COMPLETE, EXAMPLES

| Name | Schleiermacher Number | Current Location | Rider Holding | Date AD |
|---|---|---|---|---|
| Insus son of Vodullus | (none) | Lancaster | Sword & Shield | c.75-120 |
| Unknown | (none) | Ribchester | Spear & Shield | c.75-120 |
| Sextus | (71) | Chester | Spear & Shield | c. 200 |
| Dannicus | (74) | Cirencester | Spear & Shield | c.50-80 |
| Valerius Genialis | (75) | Cirencester | Spear & Standard | c.50-80 |
| Longinus Sdapeze | (76) | Colchester | Spear & Shield | c.50 |
| Flavinus | (77) | Hexham | Standard (Imago) | c.70-90 |
| Rufus Sita | (79) | Gloucester | Spear & Shield | c.50-80 |

The memorial to Longinus at Colchester Museum. Longinus Sdapeze, son of Matycus, was a *duplicarius* of the first Thracian cavalry. The *duplicarius* was a sort of non commissioned officer, the derivation of the name being that he earned double that of the ordinary trooper. Longinus, depicted wearing scale armour, lived to 40, having served for 15 years. This picture was taken in 2006, with the face, missing on first discovery of the stone in 1928, now replaced.

The four Chester 'Reiter Stones'. Though the best known of the Chester pieces the tombstone of Sextus (bottom left) is not typical of the type, featuring the image of the deceased and two lions with protruding tongues in its upper section. Furthermore, though there is a 'rider', the portrayal of the dismounted figure has been interpreted in more than one way. He may simply be a barbarian who has not fallen as yet, but it has also been suggested that he is a *calo,* or servant or slave, of Sextus. The fallen barbarian fragment (above left), numbered 551 in *Roman Inscriptions*, has been described as the finest piece of Roman sculpture in the Grosvenor collection. It shows the barbarian, armed with sword, shield and a broken lance, clinging to the leg of a cavalryman's horse. Piece number 550 in *Roman Inscriptions* (above) shows a cavalryman in mail riding over a prostrate barbarian lying face down over his shield. The fragment of the stone to Julius Severus (right) exists primarily as an inscription with the partial image of a barbarian and horses legs. It was in storage at the time of writing and is represented here by a sketch (after Schleiermacher).

The Cirencester stones. The stone of Sextus Valerius
Genialis (left), a Frisian tribesman, and trooper of the
Thracian cavalry. Genialis carries a spear and a small
standard. The less well preserved piece is a memorial
to Dannicus (above), a trooper in the *Turma* of Albanus
of the *ala Gallorum Indiana* with 16 years of service.
Dannicus was a citizen of the Raurici, whose homeland
is now part of German speaking northern Switzerland.
(Photos Corinium Museum – Cotswold District Council)

The replica of the memorial to Flavinus in the visitor centre at Corbridge Fort near Hadrian's Wall (left), and the original carving at Hexham Abbey in an old postcard illustration (right). It is thought that the memorial to Flavinus was first erected at Corbridge, a major supply depot, but it was actually discovered at Hexham Abbey in 1881 – where it still resides. Flavinus is notable as carrying a staff, or small standard, and wearing a plumed helmet. He served seven years with the *ala Petriana*, and died at the age of 25.

Replica gravestone of Flavinus, cavalryman of the ala Petriana (see reverse for details)

# Badly Degraded Examples and Fragments

| Name | Schleiermacher Number | Current Location | Rider Holding | Date AD |
|------|----------------------|------------------|---------------|---------|
| Marcus Aurelius Victor | (68) | Newcastle | Sword | c. 200-250 |
| Vitellius Tancinus | (69) | Bath | Unknown | c. 50-80 |
| Unknown | (none) | Bath | Spear & Shield | Unknown |
| Julius Severus | (70) | Chester | Unknown | After 100 |
| Unknown | (72) | Chester | Unknown | c.100-200 |
| Unknown | (73) | Chester | Spear | After 200 |
| Unknown | (78) | Dorchester | Spear & Shield | c.200-300 |
| Unknown | (80) | Carlisle | Spear & Shield | c.100-200 |
| Claudius Tirintius | (81) | Shrewsbury | Unclear | c.75-150 |
| Unknown | (82) | British Museum | Spear | c.200-400 |
| Unknown | (83) | British Museum | Sword | c.200-400 |
| Unknown | (84) | British Museum | Spear | Unknown |
| Unknown | (none) | Maryport | Sword | c.200-400 |
| Unknown | (none) | Chesters | Unknown | Unknown |

The existence of 22 British Reiter stones can clearly be demonstrated by means of the surviving material evidence. Of these 14 are either fragmentary, or very badly worn. The pieces currently in the British Museum came originally from Kirkby Thore, whilst the Carlisle example was first erected at Stanwix. Flavinus, now at Hexham Abbey is thought to have originated from Corbridge: similarly Marcus Aurelius Victor came from Chesters. Claudius Tirintius came from Wroxeter. The fragment now at Chesters showing a fallen barbarian, but little else, originated from Halton Chesters. The former existence of a few further examples, notably one from Kirkham, Lancashire, and another from Ribchester (*Roman Inscriptions of Britain* number 595), can also be deduced from the paper record.

Only eight complete or near complete pieces are known to survive, and of these six appear in the Schliermacher catalogue of 1984. Taken together the Lancaster and Ribchester memorials are thus a very significant addition to the academic canon.

The memorial to Rufus Sita, a trooper of the sixth cohort of Thracians, who died aged 40 after 22 years service. Note the apparent length of the cavalry sword or *spatha*, and the way that the horses hooves break the frame of the relief. (Gloucester City Museum)

**The three Kirkby Thore stones, now in the British Museum.**

Size, 3 feet 5 inches by 2 feet 11 inches.

Unnamed 'Reiter' stone from Kirkby Thore, (number 82 in the Schleiermacher catalogue, 756 in the *Lapidarium Septentrionale* ) now displayed in the British Museum. (Photo by Tim Padley)

Unnamed 'Reiter' (designated number 83 in the Schleiermacher catalogue, or 754 in the *Lapidarium Septentrionale)*. This rather crude piece is exceptional in that the barbarian appears prostrate with head and arms toward the viewer. It is thought to be a comparatively late carving.

Fragmentary 'Reiter' stone (number 84 in the Schleiermacher catalogue), as pictured in the *Lapidarium Septentrionale*, item 755.

Size, 2 feet 11 inches by 1 foot 10 inches.

The stone to Marcus Aurelius Victor. Discovered at Ox Close near Chesters fort in 1716. This Reiter stone is a late example, and lacks any 'fallen enemy'. The steed also resembles a mule rather than a horse. This stone is now at the Museum of Antiquities, Newcastle (number 68 in Schleiermacher; 118 in the *Lapidarium*).

The Bath 'Reiter' stones. The stone to Vitellius Tancinus, *Roman Inscriptions* 159 (right), is the better known of the Bath fragments. It records that Lucius Vitellius Tancinus was a tribesman of Caurium in Spain, and served with the Vettones. The steed features horse furniture with decorative strap ends reminiscent of the Lancaster stone. The less well known second fragment (bottom) is an upper portion of a memorial featuring a horseman with spear and shield. (Bath and North East Somerset Council)

Drawing of the remaining fragment of the memorial to Tiberius Claudius Tirintius, from Wroxeter, and now held at Rowley's House Museum, Shrewsbury. This soldier was in a partially mounted unit – or *cohors equitata* – of Thracians. He died at the age of 57. (Ben Edwards)

The 'Reiter' stone found in the wall of the church at Stanwix in 1787, later in the Netherhall collection, Maryport, and now at Tullie House Museum Carlisle. The shadowy inscription 'Dis Manibus' was identified by F. Haverfield, but there is no indication of name or unit remaining. Thought to be a late piece due to the style, which is somewhat similar to one of those from Kirkby Thore (Schleiermacher number 83, or *Lapidarium* 754). (Photo by Tim Padley)

The Maryport Reiter tombstone. Tentatively dated to 200-400 AD this piece was originally part of the old Netherhall collection. Though badly degraded, or possibly unfinished, it bears similarities to some of the other later examples. It is associated with the Roman fort at Maryport, and is now housed in the new Senhouse Museum, a converted Victorian battery beside the fort remains. (Senhouse Museum, Cumbria).

A late Roman armoured cavalryman, c.300 AD, as depicted on the Arch of Galerius, Salonika.

# Sources and Further Reading

## Books and Theses:

A.S. Anderson — *Roman Military Tombstones,* Shire Archaeology, Princes Risborough, 1984.

P. Bidwell — *Roman Forts in Britain.* English Heritage, London, 1997.

R. Birley — *The Early Wooden Forts: The Weapons.* Vindolanda Research Reports, New Series vol IV, 1996 (continuing)

M.C. Bishop & J.C. Coulston — *Roman Military Equipment*, Shire Archaeology, Princes Risborough, 1989.

M. Brennard (ed) — *The Archaeology of North West England*, Archaeology North West, vols 8 & 9, 2006 and 2007.

J. Collingwood Bruce — *Lapidarium Septentrionale: or, a Description of the Monuments of Roman Rule in the North of England*, Society of Antiquaries of Newcastle Upon Tyne, London, 1875,

P. Connolly — *Greece and Rome at War*, Macdonald Phoebus, London, 1981.

J.C. Coulston & E.J. Phillips — *Corpus Signorum Imperii Romani*, British Academy, Oxford University Press, 1977 onwards

C.M. Daniels — *Mithras and his Temples on the Wall, Museum of Antiquities*, Third Revised Edn. Newcastle, 1989.

W.F. and J.N.G. Ritchie — *Celtic Warriors*, Shire Archaeology, Princes Risborough, 1985.

M. Feugere — *Weapons of the Romans,* French edn. Paris 1993, English trans, Tempus, Stroud, 2002.

C.M. Gulliver — *The Roman Art of War*, Tempus, Stroud, 2002.

P.A. Holder — *The Roman Army in Britain*, Batsford, London, 1982.

M. Junkelmann — *Die Reiter Roms, Teil II, Der Militarische Einsatz*, Zabern, Mainz, 1991.

| N.P. Milner (ed) | *Vegetius: Epitome of Military Science,* Liverpool University Press, 1996. |
| G.J. Oliver | *The Epigraphy of Death: Studies in the History and Society of Greece and Rome,* Liverpool University, 2000. |
| B. Onken | *Wirtschaft an der Grenze Studien in den Romischen Militarlagern im Norden Britanniens,* University of Kassel, PhD thesis, 2003. |
| H.R. Robinson | *The Armour of Imperial Rome,* London, 1975. |
| P. Salway | *Roman Britain,* (Corrected edn) Oxford University, 1985. |
| M. Schleiermacher | *Romische Reitergrabsteine die Kaiserzeitlichen Reliefs des Triumphierenden Reiters,* Bouvier, Bonn, 1984. |
| W. Shannon | *The Whalley Altar: A Romano-Celtic Horned God in Heavy Cavalry Dress,* unpublished, Fulwood, 1990. |
| D.C.A. Shotter & A. White | *The Romans in Lunesdale,* Centre for North West Regional Studies, Lancaster, 1995. |
| D.C.A. Shotter | *Romans and Britons in North West England,* (Revised edn) Centre for North West Regional Studies, Lancaster, 1997. |
| I.P. Stephenson | *Roman Cavalry Equipment.* Tempus, Stroud, 2003. |
| G. Sumner | *Roman Military Clothing.* Vol 1. 100BC to AD200, Osprey, Oxford, 2002. |
| E. Swift | *Roman Dress Accessories,* Shire, Princes Risborough, 2003. |
| R.S.O. Tomlin (et al) | *Roman Inscriptions of Britain,* III, Oxford (forthcoming) |
| Sir J. Turner | *Pallas Armata. Military Essayes Of the Ancient Grecian, Roman and Modern Art of War,* Chiswell, London, 1683. |
| G. Tylden | *Horses and Saddlery,* JA Allen, AMOT, London, 1965. |
| G.R. Watson | *The Roman Soldier,* Thames and Hudson, London, 1969. |
| G. Webster | *The Roman Army,* Grosvenor Museum, Chester, 1973. |
| G. Webster | *The Roman Imperial Army,* (Second edn.) Black, London, 1979. |
| R. Wilding | *Graham Webster Gallery of Roman Stones at the Grosvenor Museum Chester,* G. Emery, Chester, 2006. |

# NEWSPAPERS AND PERIODICALS:

Anon      'Roman Horseman United with his Head', in *British Archaeology*, 56, December 2000.

Anon      'What the Romans Left Us', in *Vision*, Lancashire County Council, December, 2005.

D. Alberge      'Britain is Likely to Lose Magnificent Tombstone', in *The Times*, 9 February, 2006.

G. Cooper      'I'm No Tomb Raider', in *The Visitor*, Morecambe, 15 February, 2005.

R. Hingley      'Freedom Fighter or Tale for Romans ?', in *British Archaeology*, 83, July 2005.

V.M. Hope      'Words and Pictures: the Interpretation of Romano-Britsih Tombstones', in *Britannia*, vol 28, 1997.

A. Kirk      'What Did the Romans Do For Us ?', in *Morecambe Guardian*, 11 November, 2005.

M. Mackintosh      'The Sources of the Horseman and Fallen Enemy Motif on the Tombstones of the Western Roman Empire', in *Journal of the British Archaeological Association*, 139, 1986.

E. Mayoh       'It Should Stay Here', *Citizen*, Lancaster, 16 February, 2006.

M. Pitts       'Unique Roman Tombsone May Leave UK', in *British Archaeology*, 87, March 2006.

M. Pitts       'Tombstone Saved', in *British Archaeology*, 92, February, 2007.

D.C.A. Shotter       'Cicero and the Treveri: New Light on an Old Pun', in *Greece and Rome*, Classical Association, Cambridge, 2007, vol 54, number 1.

## PRELIMINARY REPORTS AND CORRESPONDENCE:

C. Bristow                    'Geological Note on the Roman Tombstone' (correspondence), 18 August, 2006.

B.J.N. Edwards                'Preliminary Notes on the Roman Tombstone Found in Lancaster', November, 2005.

J. Paddock                    'Note on the Helmet of Insus' (correspondence), 31 July 2007.

D. Saddington                 'Note on the Regiment on the New Lancaster Gravestone', (correspondence), 6 April, 2006.

D.C.A. Shotter                'Lancaster Roman Grave Slab' (correspondence), 25 February, 2006.

J. Truran                     'Roman Tombstone from Aldcliffe Rd, Lancaster', Conservation and Condition Report, Lancashire Conservation Studios, 8 December, 2005.

## WEB SITES

Archaeology in Europe
www.archaeology.eu.com

Caesar's Gallic Wars
www.etext.library.adelaide.edu

Council for British Archaeology
www.britarch.ac.uk

The Museum of Antiquities
museums.ncl.ac.uk

'A Rare Roman Cavalry Tombstone'
www.24hourmuseum.org.uk

Roman Britain
www.roman-britain.org

A Tussle Begins to Keep Roman Find
www.morecambetoday.co.uk/

Times on Line
www.timesonline.co.uk/

Vegetius 'De Re Militari'
www.pvv.ntnu.no/~madsb/

Vindolanda Tablets on Line
www.vindolanda.csad.ox.ac.uk/

Wigan Archaeological Society
www.wiganarchsoc.co.uk/